Life on the
BLUE PLANET

Matt Reher
Traci Dibble

Table of Contents

The Blue Planet

Our Earth is about 4.5 billion years old, and more than 7 billion people call it "home." But did you know that Earth is mostly water? In fact, about 70% of Earth is covered by **oceans**.

The Earth's oceans are the Atlantic, the Arctic, the Indian, the Southern, and the largest ocean, the Pacific.

More species of plants and animals live here than anywhere else on Earth. A species is a type of plant or animal, like the bottlenose dolphin, the humpback whale, or human beings. So far, we know of more than one million different species that call the ocean home, but scientists think there could be millions more that have yet to be found.

94% of all living things on Earth live in water.

Ocean Habitats

What is it like to live in the ocean?
The answer is different for different habitats. A **habitat** is the place in which an animal lives. A good habitat is a place where an animal can find food, stay safe, and have babies. There are many different habitats in the ocean. Two main differences are the **temperature** and the **depth** of the water.

Temperature

Water in the coldest parts of the ocean is around 28 degrees (F), which is colder than ice. Some cold ocean habitats include the Arctic and the water near Antarctica. Animals that live in this water need lots of fat and fur to stay warm.

Because ocean water is salty, oceans freeze at lower temperatures than fresh water. The freezing point of oceans is 28 degrees, while rivers and lakes that aren't salty (fresh water) freeze at 32 degrees.

■ Land
● Coral Reef
■ Warm Water Surface Temperature
■ Freezing Water Surface Temperature

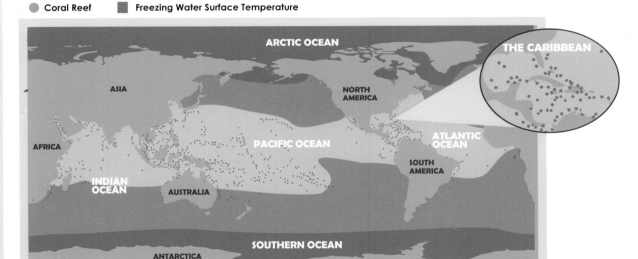

ARCTIC OCEAN

THE CARIBBEAN

ASIA

NORTH AMERICA

AFRICA

PACIFIC OCEAN

ATLANTIC OCEAN

SOUTH AMERICA

INDIAN OCEAN

AUSTRALIA

SOUTHERN OCEAN

ANTARCTICA

Water close to the middle of the earth gets lots of sun and can be up to 80 degrees, so warm it feels like a bath. Some of the warmest ocean habitats are the coral reefs of the Pacific Ocean and the water in the Caribbean.

Depth

Scientists divide the ocean into five **zones**, or parts, by the depth of the water. Ocean habitats begin on the beach, where there is very little water. The deepest parts of the ocean are 36,000 feet deep—almost 7 miles! Each zone gets different amounts of sunlight.

0 ft

650 ft

3,300 ft

13,000 ft

32,800 ft

Ocean Surface

Epipelagic Zone
(Sunlit Zone)

Mesopelagic Zone
(Twilight Zone)

Bathypelagic Zone
(Midnight Zone)

Abyssopelagic Zone
(Abyss Zone)

The deeper an animal lives in the ocean, the more water that pushes down on that animal. The weight of this push is called pressure. Pressure in the deepest parts of the ocean can reach 8 tons per square inch. That's the weight of 48 Boeing 747 jets!

Epipelagic Zone (Sunlit Zone)

All ocean plants live here because this zone gets enough sunlight for them to grow. Sharks, whales, sea turtles, and many other animals come to these warm waters to look for food.

Mesopelagic Zone (Twilight Zone)

Very little sunlight gets through to this zone.
No plants can grow here. Some animals here have large eyes to help them see through the dark waters. Squid, eels, cuttlefish, and some whales live here.

Bathypelagic Zone (Midnight Zone)

There is no sunlight in this zone.
So, some animals like the anglerfish make their own light. About 90% of the ocean is in the Midnight Zone.

Abyssopelagic Zone (Abyss Zone)

There is no light here. The water is 35 degrees, almost freezing. Animals that live here include sea spiders, blind shrimp, basket stars and tiny squids.

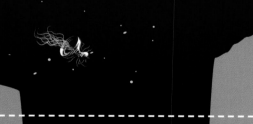

Hadalpelagic Zone (Trench Zone)

Hadalpelagic Zone (Trench Zone)

These holes, or trenches, are the deepest and coldest parts of the ocean. Starfish and tube worms are some of the only animals that can live here.

Classification

To study the millions of plants and animals that live in the ocean, scientists group them by the ways they are the same. This is called **classification**. All ocean life fits into one of these kingdoms, or categories: bacteria, fungi, protists, plants, and animals.

Bacteria

Bacteria are so tiny that you can only see them with a microscope. Some bacteria use energy from the sun to make their own food.

Fungi

Fungi are living things like mushrooms and mold. Fungi do not make their own food. They grow on and eat things like poop and dead plants and animals. Though not many fungi live in the ocean, there are ocean mushrooms and molds that grow underwater.

Protists

Protists are hard to define. The main way to define them is that they are living things in the ocean that are not bacteria, fungi, plants, or animals. The important protists in the ocean are algae. Scientists are currently arguing about what makes a protist a protist.

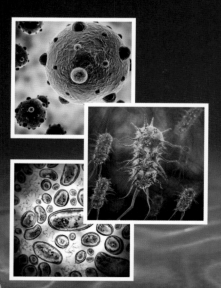

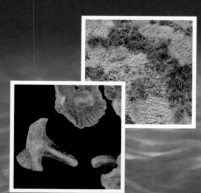

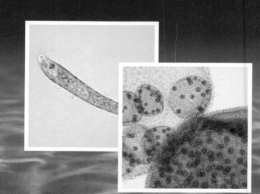

Plants

Plants are also living things that use sunlight to make their own food. However, most plants have leaves and roots, and all plants give off oxygen. Oxygen is the air that people and animals breathe to stay alive.

Animals

Animals are living things that eat plants or other animals for food. Ocean animals are separated into smaller groups based on how their bodies are shaped, how they breathe, and how they have babies.

Marine Animal Classification

Category	Mammal	Bird	Reptile
Backbone	✓	✓	✓
Body Covering	fur	feathers	scales and skin
What Type of Blood?	warm	warm	cold
How Do They Have Babies?	live birth	eggs, on land	eggs, on land or live birth, in water
How Do They Breathe?	lungs, above water	lungs, above water	lungs, above water
Unique to This Group	makes milk for babies	wings	keeps moisture in with outer skin/scales/shell
Animals in This Group	polar bears orcas seals whales sea lions manatees sea otters dolphins	seagulls penguins puffins pelicans	sea turtles sea snakes

Fish	Ocean Mollusk	Cnidarian	Crustacean
✓			
scales	soft skin	tissue around a jelly-like substance	exoskeleton
cold	cold	cold	cold
eggs or live birth, in water	eggs, in water	eggs, in water	eggs, in water
gills, underwater	gills inside their mantle cavity, underwater	diffusion (no organs)	gills, both underwater and above water
skeletons are either bone or cartilage	mantle	stinging cells	molts exoskeletons to grow
seahorses clownfish sharks rays eels	squid octopuses scallops cuttlefish	jellyfish coral anemones	crabs lobsters shrimp barnacles krill

Physical Adaptations and Survival

It's hard to make it in the ocean! Staying alive, finding food, and raising babies can be very hard in a world of giant sharks, little sun, and millions of pounds of water. Over thousands of years, ocean animals have developed special body parts and **behaviors** to help them stay alive. These are called **adaptations**.

Physical adaptations are changes to the bodies of animals. These include size, shape, color, skin covering, as well as other special body parts like sharp claws, big mouths, or long fins.

The way an animal looks may be an adaptation that helps it to hide or hunt. Some animals look like the plants, rocks, or sand in their habitats, and this allows them to hide. This is called **camouflage**. Seahorses use camouflage to hide from animals that want to eat them.

There are four kinds of camouflage.

1. **Concealing Coloration**
   Animals that are the same color as the habitat in which they live.

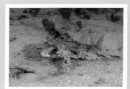
Flying Gurnard

2. **Disguise**
   Animals that blend in with their habitat because they look like other things.

Frog Fish

3. **Disruptive Coloration**
   Animals that use stripes, spots, and other patterns to blend in with their habitats.

Pygmy Seahorse

4. **Mimicry**
   Animals that look and act like other animals to trick predators.

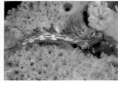
Sea Slug

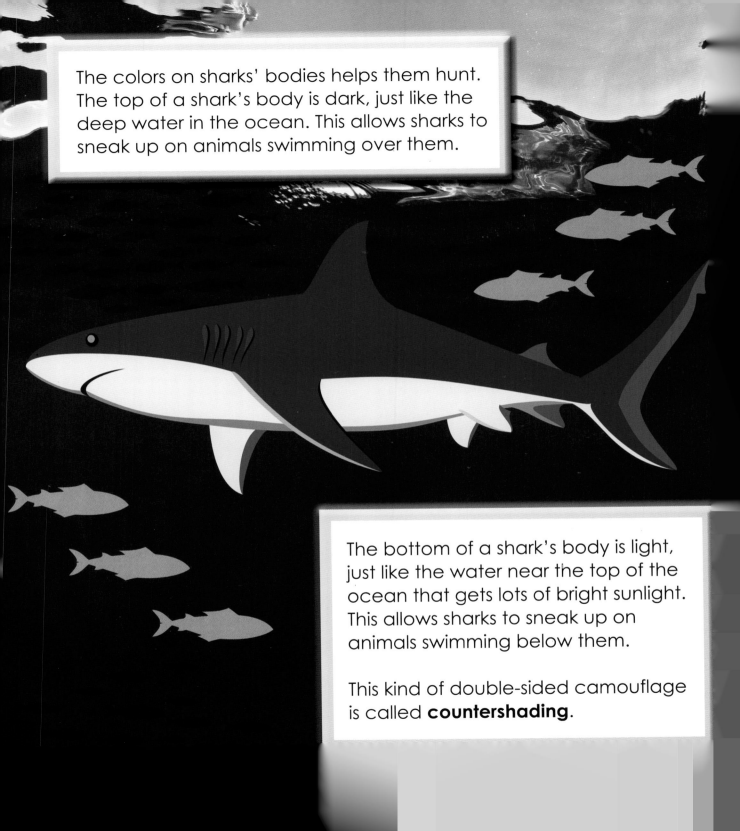

The colors on sharks' bodies helps them hunt. The top of a shark's body is dark, just like the deep water in the ocean. This allows sharks to sneak up on animals swimming over them.

The bottom of a shark's body is light, just like the water near the top of the ocean that gets lots of bright sunlight. This allows sharks to sneak up on animals swimming below them.

This kind of double-sided camouflage is called **countershading**.

Behaviors for Survival

Behavioral adaptations are changes in the way animals act. Animals behave in certain ways to stay alive, find food, and raise babies. Some animal behaviors are learned from their parents. Some behaviors animals know from birth.

For example, fish don't have to be taught to swim; they just know how to do it. This is called an **instinct**. By watching animals in their habitats, you can see the behaviors animals use to hunt, protect themselves, and raise their babies.

Some of the most interesting behavioral adaptations include different ways animals hunt. For example, humpback whales have learned to catch fish in bubbles by working as a team.

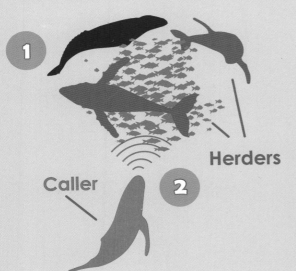

Caller

Herders

Ring Leader

1. They make a circle around a group of fish.

2. A whale dives under the fish and makes a loud sound.

3. Another whale swims above the fish and makes lots of bubbles.

4. The loud sound scares the fish, and they quickly swim up into the bubbles and get stuck.

5. Last, all the whales swim up with their mouths wide open and catch and eat the fish.

Some fish live together in large groups called schools. They do this for two reasons. First, it helps them hunt. It's much easier for a group of fish to find food this way. The second reason is that it helps them stay safe.

Many marine animals hunt little fish, and one fish swimming alone is easy to catch. When lots of little fish swim close together, they look like one big fish. This scares some large fish away.

Life Cycles

The stages living things go through during life is called a life cycle. As animals grow, there can be many new challenges to staying alive, finding food, and raising babies. Many marine animals have amazing adaptations to help them during these different stages.

LIFE CYCLE OF A SEA TURTLE

1. Egg

2. Hatchling

3. Juvenile

4. Adult

Stage 1: Laying Eggs

Sea turtles bury their eggs in the sand because it keeps the eggs warm and hides them from animals that want to eat them.

Each female lays about 110 eggs at one time and she can do this 2–8 times in one season. Not all of the baby sea turtles will live. By laying so many eggs, female sea turtles keep their species alive.

LOGGERHEAD TURTLE NESTING AREA

Eggs, Hatchlings, Adults, and Carcasses are Protected By Federal & State Laws

Contact
1-800-922-5431
www.dnr.sc.gov/seaturtle/

Stage 2: Hatchling

After 6–8 weeks, the **hatchlings**, or baby sea turtles, come out of their eggs and slowly crawl to the ocean. Many **predators** come to eat the hatchlings. Some will get eaten, but the strongest and fastest make it to the ocean.

Stage 3: Juvenile

Once in the ocean, the young sea turtles are called **juveniles**. The same long flippers that made it hard to move on sand make it easy to swim. They spend the next ten years swimming in the ocean.

Stage 4: Adulthood

When it's time for female sea turtles to lay their eggs, they amazingly go to the exact same beach where they were born. Scientists know this is an instinct because sea turtles don't learn anything from their parents. In fact, they never even meet them!

Oceans in Trouble

Sea turtles have many adaptations that help them live in the ocean, but because of people, these adaptations are not enough anymore. Most sea turtles eat ocean plants. When people spill oil or dump trash into the ocean, it can kill sea turtles' food. Without plants to eat, sea turtles are in trouble. Sea turtles are just one example of the hundreds of ocean animal and plant species that are in trouble right now. So many different living things are in trouble because everything in the ocean is connected through food chains and food webs.

Don't Splash Your Trash

SKIP THE STRAW, SAVE A SEA TURTLE

Food Chain

This picture shows one example of an ocean **food chain**. All living things need energy to live. They get energy from food. Plants make their own food from sunlight and water. Animals get energy by eating plants or animals. A food chain shows how energy moves.

For example, the plants make food from sunlight. The crab eats the plants. The octopus eats the crab. The orca eats the octopus. The sun's energy travels up through the food chain, from the sun to the orca.

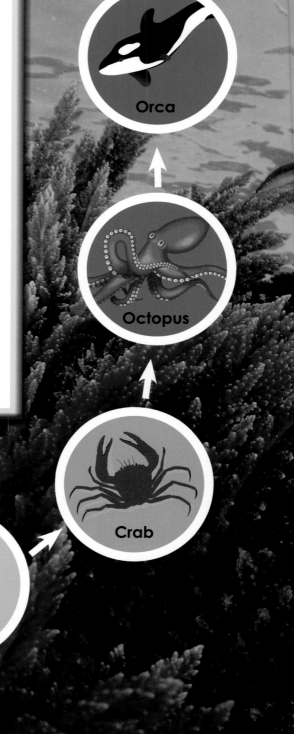

Orca

Octopus

Crab

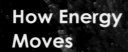

How Energy Moves

Seaweed

Sun

Food Web

A food chain is simple. Real life is not. In real life, a crab can eat seaweed, but so can a cod fish. An octopus can eat a crab, but so can a seagull. A **food web** shows how many different food chains are connected to each other. A food web also shows how many different living things need each other to survive. If one living thing in the chain is in trouble, the others are usually in trouble, too.

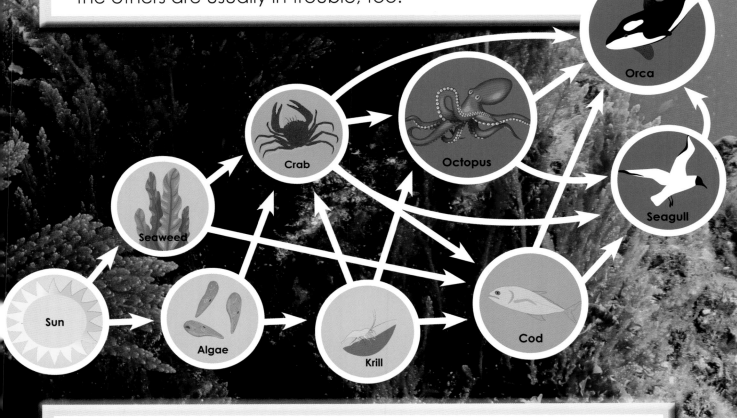

For example, if people catch too many crabs, the octopuses won't have crabs to eat. Without crabs for food, the octopuses may starve and die. Now there are less octopuses for the orcas to eat. Without octopuses to eat, the orcas may starve, too.

These changes can cause many species of plants and animals to die out and disappear forever. This is called **extinction**. Species that are in danger of going extinct are called **endangered**. Some of the ocean animals that are endangered right now are sea turtles, sea lions, Atlantic salmon, and blue whales.

Caribbean Monk Seal

Great Auk

EXTINCT

Steller's Sea Cow

Sea Lion

Atlantic Salmon

ENDANGERED

Blue Whale

Hawksbill Sea Turtle

The U.S. Government keeps a list of animal and plant species that are endangered. It also keeps a list of animal and plant species that are **threatened**, which means they aren't endangered yet, but they could be if things don't change.

Vaquita Porpoise

Staghorn Coral

Galapagos Penguin

Johnson's Seagrass

Southern Rockhopper Penguin

ENDANGERED

THREATENED

Scalloped Hammerhead Shark

Polar Bear

Banggai Cardinalfish

Largetooth Sawfish

Lots of marine life is endangered because of water **pollution**. Water pollution is any harmful thing like trash, chemicals, or oil found in the water. In 1989, an oil ship spilled enough oil in the waters of Alaska to fill 125 Olympic swimming pools. The oil killed about 300 seals, 28,000 sea otters, and 250,000 seabirds. The oil spill also killed billions of fish eggs. Because of water pollution, sea turtles, tiger sharks, and cape penguins are endangered.

Water pollution in the ocean is a big problem for all of life on Earth because more than 97% of the water on Earth is in the ocean. This means that if we pollute the water too much, we can end up without enough clean water to drink or safe fish to eat.

NO DUMPING DRAINS TO OCEAN

WARNING FISH CONTAMINATED DO NOT EAT

Another reason marine animals are endangered is overfishing. **Overfishing** is when people take fish from the ocean faster than the fish can make more fish babies. Eventually, there will be no more fish to make babies, which means no more fish.

In the last 60 years, humans have killed about 90% of the ocean's sharks, tuna, and swordfish. Humans overfish marine mammals, too. Because of overfishing, eel, sea otters, blue whales, sea bass, Atlantic cod, and bluefin tuna are endangered. Overfishing can be a big problem for humans, too. Many people around the world count on ocean plants and animals for their food. Without them, they may starve.

Manatees are at risk for a different reason: speedboats.

Manatees move slowly, and they like to swim in shallow water where they can eat sea grass. When a speedboat moves quickly through the water, manatees can't get out of the way fast enough. Many get hit. People have worked long and hard to save the manatees. As of January 2016, because of their efforts, the manatee is no longer on the endangered list.

MANATEE ZONE

SLOW SPEED

MINIMUM WAKE

Scars from propellers

People need healthy oceans for food and water. We also need healthy oceans so that we have clean air to breathe. Oceans make half of the air we breathe. Oceans also help to clean air we've already polluted. Without healthy oceans full of healthy plants and animals, humans might end up on the endangered species list!

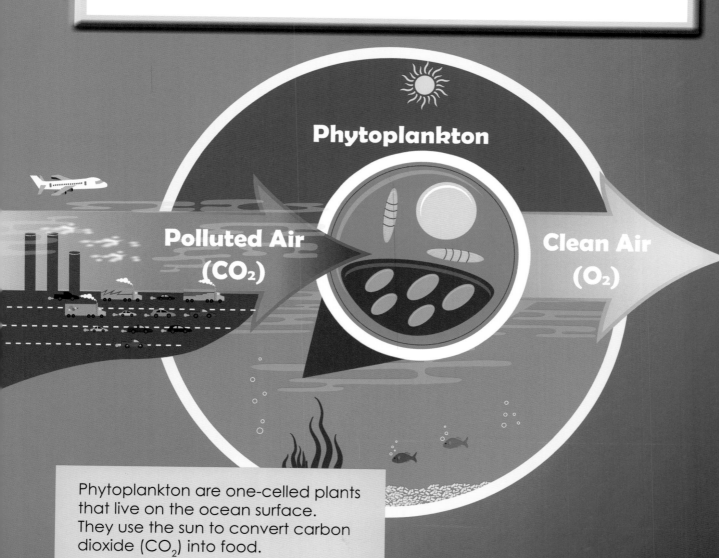

Phytoplankton

Polluted Air (CO₂)

Clean Air (O₂)

Phytoplankton are one-celled plants that live on the ocean surface. They use the sun to convert carbon dioxide (CO_2) into food.

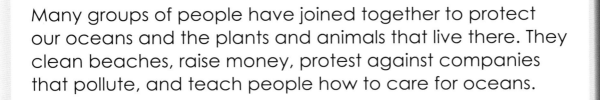

Many groups of people have joined together to protect our oceans and the plants and animals that live there. They clean beaches, raise money, protest against companies that pollute, and teach people how to care for oceans.

Some countries make laws to keep the waters clean and save the animals. Many people have stopped eating fish, or only eat fish that are caught in ways that don't hurt the oceans or the plants and animals that live there.

Sustainable Fish Farm

Our planet is nicknamed the Blue Planet because of its amazing oceans. Our oceans are part of what makes Earth so special and keeps us alive and healthy. It's important to protect them for billions of years to come.

Resources

Ocean Biome, The. Kalman, Bobbie. Crabtree Publishing, Ontario, Canada. 2003.

Endangered Oceans, Investigating Oceans in Crisis. Rake, Jody Sullivan. Capstone Press, North Mankato, MN. 2015.

http://twistedsifter.com/2010/07/15-fascinating-schools-of-fish/

https://marine-conservation.org/what-we-do/advocate/why-we-protect-our-oceans/

http://www.nda.agric.za/doaDev/sideMenu/fisheries/08_CoastCareFactSheetsSeries/docs/3A%20General%20-%20Classification.pdf

https://www.worldwildlife.org/species

http://www.nmfs.noaa.gov/pr/species/

https://www.nodc.noaa.gov/SatelliteData/Education/DLESE/2007/lesson_2007.html

http://nationalgeographic.org/activity/save-the-plankton-breathe-freely/

NOTE: At the time of printing, all of the above resources were active and accessible. Due to the transient nature of the internet, we cannot guarantee they will be available in the future.

Index

adaptation: a change in an animal or plant's genes that helps it survive where it lives

bacteria: a group of very tiny living things made of one cell without a nucleus

behavior (adapt): the way an animal moves, acts, and reacts

camouflage: the shape or color of an animal that keeps it hidden

classification (species): the way living things are divided up into groups based on their traits, genes, or family history

countershading: a kind of two-color camouflage where the animal blends into the light from underneath and blends into the dark from above

depth: the distance or area below a surface

endangered: a type of living thing at risk of dying out

extinction: when a type of living thing has died out forever

food chain: a set of animals and plants that shows "who eats what"

food web: several food chains linked together to show "who eats what" on a bigger scale

fungi: a group of living things that look a lot like plants and live on dead or decaying plants and animals